TABLE OF CONTENTS

CHAPTER ONE 7

Introduction 7

CHAPTER TWO 9

Essential tips for travelers 9

CHAPTER THREE..10

Most popular places in Egypt 10

Cairo 10

Fun places to visit in Cairo 11

Alexandria...14

Fun places to visit in Alexandria 15

Luxor 18

Places to visit in Luxor.......................................19

Aswan 21

Fun places to visit in Aswan 22

Sharm El Sheikh 24

Fun places to visit in Sharm El Sheikh 25

Dahab 27

Fun places to visit in Dahab 28

Hurghada 30

Places to visit in Hurghada 31

El Gouna 33

Places to visit in El Gouna 34

Nuweiba 36

Places to visit in Nuweiba 37

Sahl Hasheesh 39

Places to visit in Sahl Hasheesh 40

Taba 42

Places to visit in Taba 43

Marsa Alam 45

Places to visit in Marsa Alam 46

Places to visit in Siwa Oasis 49

Bahariya Oasis 51

Places to visit in Bahariya Oasis 52

Farafra Oasis 55

Places to visit in Farafra Oasis 55

Dakhla Oasis 58

Places to visit in Dakhla Oasis 59

Kharga Oasis 61

Places to visit in Kharga Oasis............................62

Suez..64

Places to visit in Suez..65

Ismailia..67

Places to visit in Ismailia 68

Port Said...70

Places to visit in Port Said 71

CHAPTER FOUR..73

Conclusion..73

CHAPTER ONE

Introduction

Egypt is a country that is known for its ancient history, stunning architecture, and awe-inspiring scenery. It is a land of contrasts, with great cities such as Cairo, Alexandria, and Luxor, and vast desert regions like the Sahara. Egypt has something for everyone, from the bustling cities to the secluded beaches, and the majestic pyramids and monuments. Whether you're looking for culture, adventure, or relaxation, Egypt has it all.

When planning a trip to Egypt, there are a few things to keep in mind. First, the country has a hot and dry climate, so it's important to bring appropriate clothing and sunscreen. Second, Egypt is a predominantly Muslim country, so it's important to be respectful of the local customs and culture. Finally, it's important to remember that Egypt is a relatively safe country, but it's still important to take precautions such as avoiding carrying large amounts of cash and not wearing flashy jewelry.

When it comes to sightseeing, Egypt has so much to offer. The most popular destinations are the Pyramids of Giza, the

Great Sphinx, and the Valley of the Kings. Other popular sites include the Temples of Luxor and Karnak, the Egyptian Museum, and the Coptic Quarter of Cairo. For a more relaxed experience, there are plenty of beaches and resorts to choose from.

Egypt is also known for its vibrant nightlife, with many bars, clubs, and restaurants to explore. There are also plenty of cultural events to enjoy, including concerts, plays, and traditional dance performances.

No matter what type of experience you're looking for, Egypt is sure to have something for you. From the ancient to the modern, from the hustle and bustle of the cities to the serenity of the desert, Egypt is sure to be an unforgettable experience because of its climate, culture, and incredible sights that inspires travelers to return again and again with their loved ones for the sweet memories and remarkable experiences.

Even with the hot weather , Egypt is still a great place to visit, so pack your bags and get ready for the journey of a lifetime with a low budget of money you can still enjoy a lot of activities and attractions in Egypt.

CHAPTER TWO

Essential tips for travelers

1. Research the city you're visiting: Before you arrive, research the city to find out what kind of activities and attractions are available. This will give you a better idea of what kind of activities you should plan for your trip.
2. Stay active: Take advantage of the city's outdoor activities such as biking, kayaking, and hiking. These activities can help you stay active while exploring the city.
3. Visit local attractions: Take time to visit the city's local attractions such as museums, parks, and landmarks.
4. Try something new: Don't be afraid to try something new. From zip-lining to hot air balloon rides, there are plenty of fun activities you can try.
5. Eat local food: Eating local food is a great way to get a taste of the culture and the local flavors.

CHAPTER THREE

Most popular places in Egypt

Cairo

With its amazing blend of ancient and modern culture, Cairo is a city that has something for everyone. From its ancient Egyptian monuments and pyramids to its vibrant nightlife and modern shopping malls, Cairo is a city that is full of surprises.

Cairo is the capital of Egypt, and it is the largest city in the country. In addition to being a major financial and political hub, Cairo is also a popular tourist destination. It is home to some of the most famous attractions in the world, including the Pyramids of Giza, the Sphinx, and the Cairo Tower. Visitors to the city can take a tour of these ancient monuments and explore the many museums, churches, and mosques that are located here.

Cairo is also known for its vibrant nightlife. The city has numerous nightclubs, bars, and music venues that offer live entertainment throughout the night. The city also has a vibrant food scene, with numerous restaurants serving a variety of cuisines. From traditional Egyptian dishes to international cuisine, Cairo has something for everyone.

Cairo is also home to a number of modern shopping malls, where visitors can find the latest fashions, electronics, and more. These malls offer a range of luxury brands and are a great place to pick up souvenirs and gifts.

When it comes to sightseeing, Cairo has plenty to offer. Visitors can take a boat ride on the Nile, explore the ancient ruins of the city, or take a guided tour of the city's many monuments and museums. There are also plenty of opportunities for outdoor activities, such as camel riding and horseback riding.

Overall, Cairo is a city with something for everyone. Whether you're looking for a cultural experience, a night out on the town, or a shopping spree, Cairo has it all. With its unique blend of ancient and modern culture, Cairo is a great place to visit and explore.

Fun places to visit in Cairo

1. Cairo Tower: This iconic landmark stands tall at 187 meters and offers beautiful views of the city. It is located in the Zamalek neighborhood and is the

tallest structure in Cairo. It is a great place to take a break and enjoy the panoramic view of the city.

2. The Pyramids of Giza: One of the Seven Wonders of the World, the Pyramids of Giza are the oldest of the ancient wonders and are the only surviving structures. It is a great place to explore the history of Egypt and take some amazing photos.

3. The Citadel of Cairo: This fortress was built in the 12th century and is one of the most impressive structures in Cairo. It is an amazing place to explore and take in the history of the city.

4. Khan el-Khalili Bazaar: This bustling market is one of the oldest in the world and is a great place to explore and experience the culture of the city. You can find all kinds of items, from souvenirs to spices and textiles.

5. The Coptic Museum: This museum is a great place to learn about the history of the Coptic Christians in Egypt. It houses a great collection of artifacts and art from the Coptic era.

6. The Egyptian Museum: Located in Tahrir Square, this museum is a must-visit for anyone interested in

learning more about the history of Egypt. It houses a vast collection of artifacts from ancient Egypt and is a great place to explore the culture and history of the country.

Alexandria

If you're looking for a fun and exciting place to visit, Alexandria, Egypt is the perfect spot for your next vacation. Situated on the Mediterranean coast, Alexandria has something for everyone. From its rich history and culture to its vibrant nightlife and beautiful beaches, a visit to this city will be sure to leave you with some unforgettable memories.

First and foremost, Alexandria is known for its ancient history and culture. As the home of the ancient Library of Alexandria, the city is full of fascinating historical attractions. Take a stroll through the old city and visit the Catacombs of Kom el Shoqafa, or marvel at the beauty of the Montazah Palace.

In addition to its many historical sites, Alexandria is also known for its vibrant nightlife. Whether you're looking for a lively club scene or a relaxing evening of wine and conversation, you'll find plenty of entertainment options in the city's many bars and restaurants. For an especially memorable evening, take an evening cruise along the harbor, where you can watch the sun set over the Mediterranean Sea.

For those who prefer to spend their time outdoors, Alexandria has some stunning beaches to explore. Head to the Corniche to experience some of the city's best beaches, or take a day trip to the nearby sandy beaches of Abu Qir and Ras el Tin. With its warm climate, Alexandria is the perfect place for a beach holiday.

No matter what type of traveler you are, Alexandria has something for everyone. From its rich history and culture to its vibrant nightlife and beautiful beaches, a visit to this city is sure to be an unforgettable experience.

Fun places to visit in Alexandria

1. Old Town Alexandria – The historic district of Alexandria offers a variety of shops, restaurants, and attractions, perfect for exploring the city's past and culture.

2. George Washington's Mount Vernon – Explore the estate of America's first president and tour the mansion, grounds, and gardens of Mount Vernon.

3. The Torpedo Factory Art Center – This art center houses over 80 studios and galleries, making it the perfect place to find unique and handmade gifts.

4. The National Inventors Hall of Fame – This Smithsonian-affiliated museum is dedicated to honoring inventors and innovators and offers interactive exhibits and events.

5. Alexandria Waterfront Park – This park offers beautiful views of the Potomac River and is a great place to enjoy a picnic or take a stroll.

6. Carlyle House Historic Park – This mansion offers a glimpse into the life of 18th-century Alexandria and features costumed interpreters and special events.

7. United States Patent and Trademark Office Museum – This museum celebrates the history of intellectual property and patent law and features interactive exhibits and artifacts.

8. Hunting Creek – This state park offers waterfront access to the Potomac River and a variety of hiking, fishing, and boating activities.
9. George Washington Masonic National Memorial – This memorial honors the legacy of George Washington and includes an observation deck with views of the city.
10. The George Washington – This luxury hotel is located in the heart of Old Town Alexandria and offers a variety of amenities and attractions.

Luxor

Luxor, Egypt is an amazing destination for anyone who loves to explore and experience the beauty and history of this ancient land. Located in the heart of the Nile Valley, Luxor offers visitors an incredible array of activities and sights to explore. From the majestic tombs of the Pharaohs to the stunning temples of the gods, Luxor is a destination that will leave you in awe and wonder.

If you're looking for a fun and exciting way to explore Luxor, you'll find plenty of activities and attractions that will keep you entertained. Start your adventure by taking a hot air balloon ride over the Valley of the Kings. Get a bird's eye view of the ancient tombs and monuments of the Pharaohs, and then float over the majestic river Nile.

For a more hands-on experience, you can take part in a camel ride through the desert. Relax and enjoy the scenery as you meander through the desert, passing by ancient ruins and oases. Be sure to stop at the Colossi of Memnon, two massive stone statues that were once part of the great temple of Amenhotep III.

If you're interested in learning more about the ancient history of Luxor, there are plenty of tour guides and museums to explore. Take a guided tour through the Valley of the Kings and learn about the powerful Pharaohs that ruled this land. Visit the Temple of Karnak and explore the spectacular columns and hieroglyphics that adorn its walls.

Luxor is also home to some of the world's best shopping and dining. Wander through the markets of Luxor and pick up souvenirs and handmade goods. Enjoy the fine cuisine of the city, from traditional Egyptian dishes to international flavors.

Whether you're looking for a fun and exciting adventure or an educational and cultural experience, Luxor has something for everyone. Come explore this ancient land and discover the many wonders and secrets that it holds.

Places to visit in Luxor

1. Valley of the Kings: Explore the ancient tombs of Pharaohs, Queens, and Nobles at this iconic site.

2. Karnak Temple: Discover the ancient temple complex of Amon, Mut and Khonsu.

3. Luxor Temple: Marvel at the grandeur of this ancient temple dedicated to Amun-Ra.

4. Luxor Museum: Learn about the ancient history of Egypt at this fascinating museum.

5. Luxor Balloon Rides: Enjoy a bird's eye view of Luxor from above as you soar in a hot air balloon.

6. Rowing on the Nile: Take a romantic cruise down the Nile River, perfect for a romantic evening.

7. Luxor Sound and Light Show: Immerse yourself in the history of Luxor as you watch the captivating sound and light show.

8. Luxor Shopping: Shop for souvenirs and gifts, or enjoy the vibrant atmosphere of the bustling markets.

9. Horse and Camel Riding: Enjoy a unique and thrilling tour of the ancient sites on horse or camel.

10. Dendara Temple: Visit the ancient temple of Hathor, goddess of love and fertility.

Aswan

Aswan is a beautiful city located in the southern part of Egypt that has a lot to offer for travelers looking for a vacation filled with fun and activities. From the majestic Nile River to the stunning desert landscape, Aswan is a place of beauty and culture that will leave you with lasting memories.

The Nile River is one of the main attractions in Aswan. You can take a cruise down the river and explore the many islands and monuments that line the river banks. Along with the beautiful views, you can also take part in activities such as fishing, swimming, and even camel rides.

If you're looking for a more cultural experience, Aswan is also home to several ancient temples and monuments. The Philae Temple is one of the most well-known monuments in Aswan and is a great place to explore and learn about ancient Egyptian history. You can also visit Edfu Temple, which is an impressive temple complex that dates back to the Ptolemaic period.

In addition to exploring the temples, you can also explore the nearby desert landscape. There are many different activities you can take part in, from sandboarding and camel rides to jeep safaris and hot air balloon rides. You can also explore the desert landscape on foot. There are several tours available that will take you to some of the most secluded and stunning areas of the desert.

For those looking for a more relaxing experience, there are also plenty of options for you in Aswan. You can take a leisurely stroll along the banks of the Nile, or you can take a boat ride and explore the many islands. You can also take a tour of the local markets and enjoy the local cuisine.

Aswan is a great place to visit for travelers looking for a vacation filled with fun and activities. From the majestic Nile River to the stunning desert landscape, Aswan has something for everyone. Whether you're looking for a cultural experience or a relaxing getaway, Aswan is sure to leave you with lasting memories.

Fun places to visit in Aswan

1. Philae Temple: an ancient temple complex located on the island of Agilika in the Nile River.
2. Nubian Museum: a museum dedicated to the culture and history of the Nubian people.

3. Aswan High Dam: a major engineering achievement that helps provide water and electricity to the region.
4. Unfinished Obelisk: a large piece of granite that was left unfinished due to a flaw in the stone.
5. Elephantine Island: a large island in the Nile River with ancient ruins and temples.
6. Kalabsha Temple: an ancient temple dedicated to the Nubian god Mandulis.
7. Abu Simbel: a temple complex that was carved into a mountainside in the 13th century BC.
8. Tombs of the Nobles: a series of tombs carved into the cliffs of the West Bank of Aswan.
9. Felucca Cruise: a relaxing boat ride on the Nile River.
10. Kitchener's Island: a botanical garden with a variety of rare plants and trees.

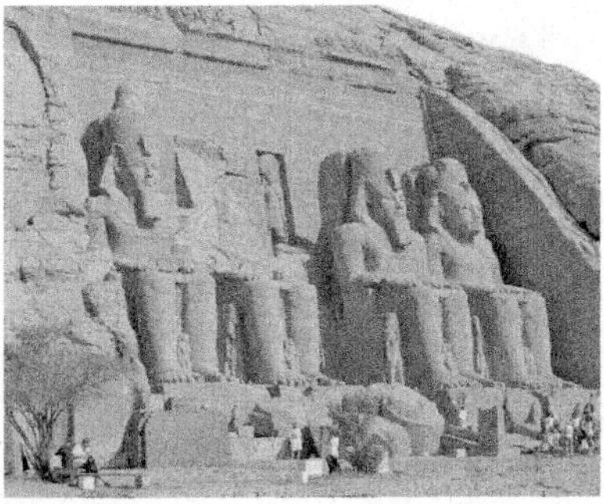

Sharm El Sheikh

If you're looking for a vacation destination that offers sun, sand and adventure, then Sharm El Sheikh is the perfect place for you. Located in Egypt's Sinai Peninsula, Sharm El Sheikh is a popular destination for both tourists and locals alike.

The city is known for its stunning beaches and crystal clear waters, making it the perfect place to relax and enjoy the sun. Whether you're looking for a romantic getaway, a family trip, or a solo adventure, Sharm El Sheikh has something for everyone.

The city is also home to some of the world's best snorkeling and diving spots, offering a range of exciting water activities. From deep sea coral diving to exotic fish spotting, the underwater world of Sharm El Sheikh is sure to captivate you.

The city also has plenty of attractions to explore. From the bustling markets to the ancient temples, there's something for everyone to discover. From camel rides to sandboarding, there's no shortage of fun activities to try.

If you're looking for a break from the beach, then head to the nearby Old Town for a taste of traditional Egyptian culture. Here you can explore the winding streets, take in the vibrant atmosphere, and sample some of the local cuisine.

Sharm El Sheikh is the perfect destination for travelers looking for a sun-filled getaway with plenty of activities to keep you busy. Whether you're looking for relaxation or adventure, you're sure to find it in this beautiful

Fun places to visit in Sharm El Sheikh

1. Naama Bay: Enjoy a stroll along the promenade, visit the designer shops, and relax in one of the many beachfront cafes.
2. Ras Mohammed National Park: Explore the magical underwater world and admire the coral reefs and marine life.
3. Soho Square: Enjoy a variety of activities such as shopping, dining, and entertainment.
4. St. Catherine's Monastery: Explore the world's oldest Christian monastery nestled in the Sinai Mountains.

5. Mount Sinai: Climb the mountain and see the spectacular sunrise from the summit.
6. Colored Canyon: Enjoy a hike through the towering sandstone formations and explore the hidden colored caves.
7. Tiran Island: Snorkel in the crystal-clear waters and explore the vibrant coral reefs.
8. Blue Hole: Dive into the mysterious and beautiful lagoon and explore the underwater caves.
9. Star Gazing: Enjoy a night of star-gazing in the clear desert skies.
10. Quad Bike Safari: Explore the desert terrain and witness the beautiful Bedouin villages.

Dahab

Welcome to Dahab, Egypt – the perfect destination for travelers looking to explore the beautiful Red Sea and enjoy the incredible activities it has to offer. From snorkeling and diving to windsurfing and kitesurfing, Dahab is the perfect destination for fun-seekers and adventurers alike.

Dahab is known for its clear waters, colorful coral reefs, and breathtaking views of the Sinai Desert. It's a great place for diving and snorkeling, as the waters are calm and the visibility is excellent. Whether you're a beginner or a seasoned diver, you'll find plenty of dive sites to explore.

If you're looking for a more adrenaline-filled experience, Dahab is also a great spot for windsurfing and kitesurfing. You can rent equipment from local shops and explore the coast of the Red Sea. The winds in Dahab are strong and steady, perfect for both beginner and advanced riders.

If you're looking to enjoy a relaxing day on the beach, you'll find plenty of options in Dahab. The white sand beaches are perfect for sunbathing and watching the dolphins that often swim close to shore. You can also head out on a boat tour and explore the stunning coastline.

If you're looking for a more cultural experience, head to the nearby Bedouin villages. Here, you'll have the chance to learn about Bedouin culture and try local delicacies.

No matter what activities you're looking for, Dahab has something for everyone. Whether you're looking to explore the depths of the Red Sea or simply relax on the beach, you'll find plenty of things to do in Dahab. So come to Dahab and enjoy an unforgettable vacation!

Fun places to visit in Dahab

1. Blue Hole: The world-famous Blue Hole is one of the top diving destinations in the world and a must-visit in Dahab.
2. Eel Garden: The Eel Garden is home to a variety of coral and marine life, as well as a large population of friendly moray eels.
3. Lighthouse: A lighthouse standing atop a small rocky island located off the coast of Dahab. It is

accessible by boat and provides stunning views of the Red Sea.

4. Canyon: The Canyon is a unique natural formation located in the desert outside of the city. It is popular for canyoning and is a great place to explore the desert.
5. Bedouin Market: The Bedouin Market is a great place to shop for souvenirs and experience the traditional culture of the Bedouin people.
6. Camel Riding: Take a camel ride along the beach or through the desert and enjoy the beautiful scenery of Dahab.
7. Safari Trip: Go on a safari trip to explore the desert and experience the wildlife of Dahab.
8. Nightlife: Experience the vibrant nightlife of Dahab, with plenty of bars and clubs to choose from.
9. Windsurfing: Enjoy the perfect windsurfing conditions of Dahab and take in the stunning views of the Red Sea.

10. Snorkelling: Explore the underwater world of Dahab with a snorkelling trip and see a variety of colourful fish and coral.

Hurghada

Are you looking to experience the beauty of the Red Sea and the Sinai Peninsula? Then Hurghada, Egypt, is the perfect destination for your next vacation. Located on the Red Sea coast, Hurghada is a world-class resort and a popular tourist destination.

If you're a beach person, you'll love Hurghada. With its beautiful coral reefs and pristine white sand beaches, you'll be able to enjoy the sun, sea, and sand in style. Whether you're looking for a romantic getaway or a fun family vacation, Hurghada has something to offer.

For an added dose of adventure, why not take a boat trip out to the Red Sea to explore the stunning marine life? Snorkeling and scuba diving are popular activities, with plenty of opportunities to spot some of the area's colorful fish and coral.

For a more relaxed experience, take a stroll along the promenade or explore one of the many souks in town. You can also visit some of the nearby archaeological sites and learn about the area's fascinating history. Don't forget to try some of the local cuisine, too – Hurghada's restaurants serve up delicious Egyptian and international dishes.

Of course, Hurghada has plenty of accommodation options, ranging from budget guesthouses to luxury resorts. Whatever your holiday style and budget, you'll be able to find the perfect place to stay.

So if you're looking for an exciting vacation destination with plenty to see and do, look no further than Hurghada, Egypt. With its stunning beaches, fascinating history, and delicious cuisine, Hurghada is sure to be an unforgettable experience

Places to visit in Hurghada

1. Abu Minkar Palace: Visit the historical palace and its gardens, which was built in the 19th century by an Ottoman ruler.

2. Sahl Hasheesh: Enjoy the luxury of the Red Sea Riviera and its beautiful beaches. Take part in activities such as kite surfing and horseback riding.
3. Desert Safari: Take an exciting desert safari and explore the beauty of the desert. Enjoy quad biking and dune bashing, sandboarding and camel riding.
4. Hurghada Marina: Take a boat tour around the marina and see the amazing variety of yachts and boats. Enjoy the sunset and the city's skyline.
5. Sand City: Spend a day at the sand city, sliding down huge sand dunes and competing in different sports.
6. Magawish Village: Visit a traditional fishing village and explore its local culture. Go on a boat tour and enjoy the views.
7. El Gouna: Take a day trip to El Gouna, one of Egypt's most popular destinations. Enjoy its beach resorts, golf courses and marina.
8. Mahmya Island: Take a boat trip to Mahmya Island and explore its diverse wildlife. Take part in activities such as snorkelling, fishing and sailing.

9. Dolphin World: Visit Dolphin World and swim with the dolphins in their natural habitat. Enjoy other activities such as kayaking, parasailing and water skiing.

El Gouna

This vibrant city on the Red Sea coast offers a unique blend of culture, cuisine, and activities that will make your vacation truly special.

El Gouna is known as "The Pearl of the Red Sea" and it's easy to see why. With its stunning beaches, crystal-clear waters, and vibrant nightlife, it's a paradise for beach-goers, sun-seekers, and party-goers alike. Whether you're looking for a romantic getaway, an action-packed adventure, or a relaxing retreat, El Gouna has something for everyone.

The city is home to a variety of activities to keep you entertained during your stay. From water sports like snorkeling and scuba diving to beach volleyball and kite surfing, there's plenty to do in and around the water. You can also explore the local culture with a visit to the El Gouna Museum or the historic old town.

And when it's time to relax, you can take a stroll along the marina or indulge in some of El Gouna's renowned spa treatments. After dark, the city comes alive with its lively nightlife, featuring a range of bars, clubs, and restaurants.

No matter what kind of vacation experience you're looking for, El Gouna has it all. With its stunning scenery, vibrant culture, and endless activities, it's the perfect destination for beach-goers, sun-seekers, and party-goers alike. So what are you waiting for? Pack your bags and head to El Gouna for the ultimate holiday experience.

Places to visit in El Gouna

1. Mangroovy Beach: This is a beautiful beach located in El Gouna that features crystal-clear water and white sand. It is ideal for relaxing and swimming.
2. El Gouna Marina: This is a marina located in El Gouna that features a wide variety of boats and yachts for rent. It is a great place to explore the Red Sea and the surrounding islands.

3. Abu Tig Marina: This is a small marina located in El Gouna that features a variety of restaurants and bars. It is a great place to enjoy a night out and explore the local culture.

4. El Gouna Golf Course: This is a championship-level golf course located in El Gouna that features 18 holes of golf. It is a great place to practice your golf game and take in the amazing views of the Red Sea.

5. El Gouna Town Centre: This is a vibrant town centre located in El Gouna that features a variety of shops, restaurants, and cafes. It is a great place to explore the local culture and attractions.

6. El Gouna Aquarium: This is a large aquarium located in El Gouna that features a variety of marine life from the Red Sea. It is a great place to learn about the local marine life and the importance of the Red Sea.

Nuweiba

Nuweiba is an incredible destination for travelers looking for a unique, fun-filled vacation. Located on Egypt's Sinai Peninsula, Nuweiba offers picturesque beaches, lush forests, and spectacular views of the Red Sea. Whether you're looking to soak up the sun, explore the historical and cultural attractions, or take in the local culture, Nuweiba has something for everyone.

The beaches in Nuweiba are some of the most beautiful in the world. The crystal-clear waters of the Red Sea provide an ideal setting for snorkeling, swimming, and other water activities. The area is also home to some of the best coral reefs in the world, making it a great spot for scuba-diving and exploring the underwater world.

For those looking to explore the historical and cultural attractions, Nuweiba offers a wealth of sites to explore. From ancient monasteries to stunning mosques, there's something for everyone in Nuweiba. The area is also home to some of the most impressive archaeological sites in the Middle East, including the ancient city of Serabit el-Khadim and the ruins of the Temple of Hathor.

In addition to its historical and cultural attractions, Nuweiba offers a wealth of fun activities. From shopping and dining to sailing and windsurfing, there's something for everyone to enjoy. The local markets and bazaars offer a unique shopping experience, while the restaurants and cafes provide delicious local cuisine. Additionally, the area is home to a number of cultural festivals and events, making it a great spot for a fun-filled vacation.

Whether you're looking for a relaxing beach vacation or an exciting adventure, Nuweiba has something for everyone. With its stunning beaches, lush forests, and cultural attractions, Nuweiba is a truly unique destination that offers an unforgettable experience. So don't wait any longer – come and explore the wonders of Nuweiba!

Places to visit in Nuweiba

1. Nuweiba Beach: Enjoy the stunning views of the Red Sea and take part in the many water sports activities.

2. Ras Abu Galum Nature Reserve: Enjoy the natural beauty of this protected area and take a boat ride to explore the coral reefs.

3. Colored Canyon: Hike through the beautiful canyon and explore the unique landscape.

4. St. Catherine's Monastery: Visit the ancient monastery located at the base of Mount Sinai.

5. Wadi Watir: Take a walk or jeep tour through the wadi and take in the stunning views of the desert.

6. Nuweiba Castle: Visit the remains of the ancient castle and learn about its history.

7. Nuweiba Port: Take a boat ride to the offshore islands and explore the local culture.

8. Dolphin Reef: Go snorkeling and enjoy the colorful fish and reefs.

9. Bedouin Village: Visit a traditional Bedouin village and learn about their culture and customs.

10. Nuweiba Desert Safari: Take a camel ride through the desert and enjoy the sights and sounds of the desert.

Sahl Hasheesh

If you're looking for a destination that combines modern luxury and ancient culture, then Sahl Hasheesh is the perfect place for you. This stunning resort town is located on Egypt's Red Sea Coast and is known for its pristine beaches and luxurious resorts.

The town of Sahl Hasheesh is a world-class destination that is perfect for both relaxation and exploration. With its crystal-clear turquoise waters, white sand beaches and lush greenery, it's easy to see why this destination is a favorite for luxury travelers. Spend your days lounging in the sun at one of the many beach resorts and spas, or take a dip in the warm waters of the Red Sea.

If you're looking for a little adventure, Sahl Hasheesh has plenty to offer as well. Take a boat tour of the nearby coral reefs, explore the ancient ruins of the nearby city of Ptolemais or go on a desert safari. No matter what kind of experience you're looking for, Sahl Hasheesh has something for everyone.

As you explore the town, take some time to appreciate the cultural and historic sites that make Sahl Hasheesh unique.

From the vibrant Souk market to the mosques and temples, there's something special to be found around every corner.

At the end of the day, relax and unwind at one of the many fine restaurants and bars. With its high-end cuisine, international flavors and stunning views, Sahl Hasheesh is the perfect place to end your day.

No matter what kind of vacation you're looking for, Sahl Hasheesh has something for everyone. Whether you're looking for a relaxing beach retreat or an exciting adventure, this destination is sure to offer an unforgettable experience.

Places to visit in Sahl Hasheesh

1. Sahl Hasheesh Beach: This beautiful beach is perfect for sunbathing, swimming, and snorkeling. It also offers great opportunities for water sports such as windsurfing, kiteboarding, and paddle boarding.
2. Sahl Hasheesh Promenade: This promenade is a popular spot for walking, running, and cycling. It also offers great views of the Red Sea and has many restaurants and cafes.

3. Old Town: The Old Town is a great spot to explore and take in the culture of the area. It has many traditional buildings, shops, and restaurants.
4. PGA Sultan Golf Course: This 18-hole championship golf course is a great spot for golfers of all levels. It also has a driving range and clubhouse.
5. Bedouin Village: This traditional village offers a glimpse into the culture of the Bedouins that live in the area. It has many shops where you can purchase traditional items and a great selection of restaurants.
6. Aqua Park: This water park is a great spot for families and thrill seekers alike. It has a wave pool, lazy river, and many water slides.

Taba

The city of Taba in Egypt is a great place to visit for those looking for a fun and exciting vacation. Whether you are looking for some outdoor activities or an evening of relaxation, Taba has something for everyone.

Taba is located in the south of the Sinai Peninsula, bordering both Israel and the Red Sea. This makes it ideal for beach activities such as snorkeling, swimming, and windsurfing. The area is also known for its excellent diving spots with some of the most spectacular coral reefs in the world. If you're feeling adventurous, you can even go on a camel ride through the desert.

In addition to outdoor activities, Taba has plenty of shopping opportunities. There are several markets where you can purchase souvenirs and traditional Egyptian goods. The city also has several small shops and boutiques where you can shop for clothing and jewelry.

If you're looking for a more relaxed evening, there are plenty of restaurants and bars in Taba. You can enjoy a variety of delicious cuisines and a wide selection of drinks.

After dinner, you can take a stroll along the beach and enjoy the incredible views of the Red Sea.

Taba is a great destination for those looking for a fun and exciting vacation. With its variety of activities, shopping opportunities, and restaurants, it's the perfect place to visit for a memorable holiday.

Places to visit in Taba

1. Coral Beach: This is a beautiful beach with crystal-clear waters and coral reefs, perfect for swimming, snorkeling, and scuba diving.
2. Mount Sinai: This is a major religious site for both Christians and Muslims, and it is where Moses is said to have received the Ten Commandments.
3. Taba Heights: This resort town is located on a cliff overlooking the Red Sea and offers numerous activities such as golf, tennis, and beach sports.
4. Taba Museum: This museum contains artifacts from ancient Egypt and offers a great insight into the region's history.

5. Sinai Desert: This desert is perfect for those who want to explore the beauty of the region, with its stunning landscapes and unique wildlife.
6. Colored Canyon: This is a series of rock formations and canyons that offer magnificent views of the desert.
7. Pharaoh's Island: This island is located in the middle of the Red Sea and is a great spot for swimming, diving, and snorkeling.
8. St. Catherine's Monastery: This is an ancient Christian monastery located in the Sinai Mountains and is a popular tourist destination

Marsa Alam

If you're looking for a unique holiday destination with plenty of exciting activities to keep you entertained, then look no further than Marsa Alam. Located on the Red Sea coast of Egypt, Marsa Alam offers a unique blend of culture, history and natural beauty.

The main attraction in Marsa Alam is its stunning beaches. With crystal clear waters and white sand, the beaches are perfect for swimming, snorkelling or just relaxing in the sun. You'll also find plenty of other water sports to enjoy, such as windsurfing, diving and sailing.

For a more cultural experience, visit the ancient city of Marsa Alam. This city was once an important port in the Roman and Byzantine eras, and today it's a popular tourist attraction. Here you can explore the ancient ruins and visit the nearby museum to learn more about the city's past.

If you're looking for a more active holiday, there are plenty of outdoor activities in Marsa Alam. Go on a jeep safari and explore the desert. Or take a boat trip and explore a variety of secluded coves and beaches. There are also plenty of hiking trails and nature reserves to explore, allowing you to discover the stunning landscapes of the region.

Finally, if you're looking for a unique shopping experience, Marsa Alam has plenty of markets and bazaars. Here you can find a variety of traditional items, from handmade textiles to jewellery. Plus, the city is home to a number of art galleries, where you can find traditional paintings and sculptures.

For a unique holiday destination with plenty of activities to keep you entertained, then Marsa Alam is the perfect place for you. With its stunning beaches, cultural sites, outdoor activities and markets.

Places to visit in Marsa Alam

1. Marsa Alam Beach: Located along the Red Sea, Marsa Alam Beach is a popular beach destination for tourists looking to soak up the sun and take part in water activities such as swimming, snorkeling, and scuba diving.
2. Marsa Shagra Village: This traditional fishing village is a great place to explore and learn about the culture of

the locals. Visitors can participate in activities such as fishing, swimming, and taking a boat trip along the Red Sea.

3. Wadi El Gemal National Park: This national park is home to a variety of wildlife, including birds, fish, mammals, and reptiles. Visitors can take part in activities such as hiking, camel riding, and 4x4 safaris.

4. El Quseir Old Town: This old town is a great place to explore and learn about the history of the area. Visitors can take part in activities such as visiting the local market, exploring the traditional buildings, or visiting the old fort.

5. Dolphin House Reef: This reef is one of the best spots for snorkeling and diving. Visitors can see a variety of marine life and coral formations.

6. Gebel Elba National Park: This national park boasts a variety of landscapes such as mountains, valleys, and canyons. Visitors can take part in activities such as hiking, mountain biking, and camel riding.

7. Abu Dabab Beach: This beach is known for its abundance of sea turtles and dugong. Visitors can take part in activities such as as swimming, snorkeling, and

scuba diving. 8. St. Anthony's Monastery: This monastery is one of the oldest in the area and is a great place to explore and learn about the history of the area. Visitors can take part in activities such as visiting the monastery, exploring the gardens, or visiting the old church. Siwa Oasis If you're looking for a unique and exotic destination for your next vacation, look no further than Siwa Oasis in Egypt. Located in the heart of the Western Desert, Siwa is a stunning oasis full of fascinating activities and breathtaking landscapes. Siwa is known for its majestic sand dunes and palm groves, which make for a great backdrop for activities like camel rides. You can take a leisurely ride through the desert, admiring the beautiful desert sunset and taking in the unique sights and sounds of the area. In addition to camel rides, Siwa also offers visitors a range of other activities to explore. The area is home to several ancient ruins, including the Temple of the Oracle and the Temple of the Sun, which are great places to explore and learn about the history of the region. Another popular activity is mountain biking, with many trails running through the oasis. For those who love a challenge, there is also a 4x4 off-road tour of the oasis, which is an unforgettable experience. If you're looking to relax, Siwa also has plenty to offer. There are several spas and hot springs in the area, perfect for unwinding after a long day of exploring. The area is also home to many traditional Bedouin villages, where you can experience the culture and hospitality of the locals. No matter your interests, Siwa has something for everyone. Whether you're looking for adventure or relaxation, Siwa offers a unique and unforgettable experience. So, pack your bags and head to the desert for a vacation you won't soon forget.

Places to visit in Siwa Oasis

1. Siwa Lake: Situated in the beautiful Siwa Oasis, Siwa Lake is a popular spot for tourists who want to go swimming and enjoy the stunning natural scenery. The lake is also known for its therapeutic mud baths and healing properties.

2. Siwa House Museum: This museum is a great place to get to know the history and culture of the Siwa Oasis. It

displays an array of artifacts, including jewelry and handicrafts, as well as traditional clothing and weaponry.

3. The Great Sand Sea: This stunning desert landscape stretches all the way to the Libyan border, and is a great place to go dune bashing and explore the vast expanse of sand.

4. Bir Wahed: This is an ancient spring-fed lake located in the heart of the Siwa Oasis. It's a great spot for swimming and sunbathing, or just to relax and take in the views.

5. Siwa Shali: This small fortress town is located within the oasis and is known for its unique architecture. It's also a great spot for shopping for souvenirs and traditional handicrafts.

6. Cleopatra's Bath: This natural spring is said to be the same one used by Cleopatra herself. It's a great place to go for a refreshing swim or just to relax and take in the stunning natural views.

7. Temple of the Oracle: This ancient temple is believed to be where Alexander the Great consulted the Oracle of

Siwa about his future. It's a great place for curious tourists to explore and discover more about the history of the region

Bahariya Oasis

If you're looking for a fun and unique destination to visit, then the Bahariya Oasis should be at the top of your list. Located in the Western Desert of Egypt, the Bahariya Oasis offers an array of activities and experiences to make your trip an unforgettable one. First and foremost, the Bahariya Oasis is an ideal destination for those who love to explore the great outdoors.

With its stunning desert landscapes, it's a great place to go hiking, camping, and even sandboarding. And if you're looking for a unique experience, you can even take a camel ride and explore the desert on the back of a one-humped dromedary.

The Bahariya Oasis also offers a wide range of water activities, from swimming and snorkeling in the crystal clear waters of the oasis to kayaking and paddle-boarding. You can also explore the famous White Desert, a stunning landscape of white chalk formations and limestone rocks.

The White Desert is a great place for a romantic stargazing experience or just a peaceful stroll. If you're looking for a cultural experience, the Bahariya Oasis offers plenty of opportunities to learn about the local history and culture. Visit the ancient Roman ruins of Ain El-Muftella, and explore the ruins of the ancient city of Bawiti.

The Bahariya Oasis also offers a great selection of local restaurants, serving up traditional dishes from the region that you won't find anywhere else.

The Bahariya Oasis is the perfect destination for anyone looking for an unforgettable experience. Whether you're looking for outdoor activities or a cultural experience, the Bahariya Oasis has something for everyone. Explore the wonders of the Western Desert of Egypt and make your trip a memorable one.

Places to visit in Bahariya Oasis

1. Black Desert: The Black Desert is a unique desert landscape in the Bahariya Oasis that has been formed by a combination of iron and manganese. It is a great place for tourists to explore and take in the beauty of the desert.

2. White Desert: The White Desert is one of the most striking and unique landscapes in the Bahariya Oasis. It is made up of limestone formations, sandstone and chalk rocks, and is great for taking pictures and exploring the area.

3. El-Hamimat Natural Hot Springs: El-Hamimat Natural Hot Springs is a great spot for tourists to relax and enjoy the therapeutic benefits of hot springs. The area is known for its therapeutic healing properties and is a great place to unwind and relax.

4. El-Mufid Cave: El-Mufid Cave is an ancient limestone cave located in the Bahariya Oasis. It is a great place to explore and take in the beauty of the desert.

5. Al-Bawiti: Al-Bawiti is a small town in the Bahariya Oasis. It is a great place for tourists to explore and experience the unique culture and lifestyle of the area.

6. Bahariya Oasis Museum: The Bahariya Oasis Museum is a great place for tourists to learn about the history of the area. It contains artifacts and information about the history and culture of the oasis.

7. Valley of the Golden Mummies: The Valley of the Golden Mummies is a unique site in the Bahariya Oasis. It is a great place to explore and take in the history of the area.

8. Siwa Oasis: The Siwa Oasis is a great place for tourists to explore and visit. It is known for its natural beauty and is a great place to relax and enjoy the scenery.

9. El-Fayoum: El-Fayoum is a great spot for tourists to explore the many attractions and activities in the area. It is known for its lakes, temples and monuments, making it a great place for tourists to explore.

10. The Great Sand Sea: The Great Sand Sea is a great place for tourists to explore and take in the beauty of the desert. It is a great place to take pictures and experience the unique landscape of the area.

Farafra Oasis

Farafra Oasis has plenty to offer. From camel riding to sand-boarding, there are plenty of activities to keep you entertained. You can also explore the many ancient sites, such as the ancient Roman ruins of Qasr Farafra or the beautiful White Desert. When it comes to accommodation, Farafra Oasis is well equipped with a variety of lodges and hotels. Whether you're looking for a luxurious stay or a budget-friendly option, there's something for everyone.

No matter what you're looking for, Farafra Oasis is the perfect destination for an exciting and memorable experience. From its crystal-clear waters to its unique wildlife, the oasis offers something for everyone. So, why not book a trip to Farafra Oasis and make lasting memories?

Places to visit in Farafra Oasis

1. White Desert: It is one of the most beautiful deserts in the world and it is a perfect place for a tourist to go for fun activities such as camel rides, sandboarding, and stargazing under the night sky.

2. Farafra Oasis Hot Springs: The hot springs are located in the desert and they are a great spot to spend a day relaxing and unwinding.

3. Dakhla Oasis: This oasis is located nearby and it offers plenty of activities for tourists, including swimming, birdwatching, and visiting the local market.

4. Qasr El Labeka: This old castle is an interesting place to visit, especially for those interested in Egyptian history.

5. Al-Ghadir Mosque: This mosque is an important religious site and is worth visiting for its architecture and its spiritual atmosphere.

6. Ain Dalla: This is a natural hot spring located in the desert. It is a great spot for swimming and relaxing.

7. Great Sand Sea: This is a vast desert region filled with sand dunes and is perfect for adventurous activities such as sandboarding and off-roading.

8. El-Quseir: This is a nearby city that offers plenty of attractions, including beaches, ancient ruins, and markets.

9. Black Desert: This is a unique desert filled with black volcanic rocks and it is a great spot for hiking and exploring.

10. Local Markets: There are many interesting markets in Farafra Oasis where tourists can buy souvenirs and experience the local culture.

Dakhla Oasis

Welcome to Dakhla Oasis! This unique and special place offers a wealth of activities and sights to explore. Located in Egypt's Western Desert.

It is known for its palm groves, colorful homes, and peaceful atmosphere. The oasis is home to many Bedouin villages and is full of culture and history. The area is full of interesting activities to explore. Visitors can take part in camel safaris to explore the desert and its wildlife.

There is also an abundance of archaeological sites and ruins to check out. The area is also great for bird watching and photography. If you are looking for some adventure, Dakhla Oasis is the perfect place.

There are many activities to keep you busy, including sandboarding, kitesurfing, and kayaking. Whether you are a beginner or an expert, you will find something to challenge you. The oasis is also a great place to relax and unwind. There are several hot springs to soak in and take in the beauty of the desert.

You can also take part in traditional Bedouin activities and enjoy the local cuisine. Whether you are looking for adventure or relaxation, Dakhla Oasis has something to offer everyone. With its stunning landscapes, rich culture, and abundance of activities.

Places to visit in Dakhla Oasis

1. Al Qasr: Al Qasr is a small village situated in the middle of the Dakhla Oasis. It is known for its vibrant markets and diverse culture, and is a great place to explore and learn about the local history and culture. There are plenty of activities to do here, such as shopping in the markets, visiting the mosques, and exploring the nearby mountains.

2. Abou Mingar: Abou Mingar is a small village located in the middle of the Dakhla Oasis. This village is known for its beautiful architecture and desert landscape, and is a great place to explore the traditional Bedouin culture. There are plenty of activities to do here, such as camel and horse riding, sandboarding, and enjoying the nightlife.

3. The White Desert: The White Desert is a unique landscape located in the middle of the Dakhla Oasis. It is characterized by its white sand and rock formations,

and is a great place to explore and take pictures. There are plenty of activities to do here, such as trekking, camping, and bird watching.

4. Ain Khadra: Ain Khadra is an oasis located in the middle of the Dakhla Oasis. It is known for its lush green oasis and palm trees, and is a great place to relax and enjoy the scenery. There are plenty of activities to do here, such as swimming, fishing, and exploring the nearby ruins.

5. Dakhla Museum: The Dakhla Museum is a small museum located in the middle of the Dakhla Oasis. It is known for its collection of artifacts and historical objects from the region, and is a great place to learn about the local culture and history. There are plenty of activities to do here, such as visiting the exhibits, attending lectures, and viewing the artifacts.

Kharga Oasis

Looking for a unique and exciting destination to visit in Egypt, then Kharga Oasis is a great choice. Located in the western desert region of Egypt, the oasis is a perfect getaway for a weekend or holiday.

From sand dunes to ancient ruins, the area offers a variety of activities for tourists of all interests and ages. For the adventurous traveler, Kharga Oasis has a lot to offer.

One of the most popular activities is dune surfing, which is a great way to explore the desert and experience the thrilling rush of the wind and sand. Camel riding is also popular, allowing visitors to take in the stunning views of the desert while riding atop a gentle and majestic animal.

Those wanting a more relaxed trip can enjoy the numerous cultural sites in the area. Here, visitors can explore the ruins of ancient temples, tombs and fortresses. The area is also home to many hot springs, which provide a relaxing and therapeutic experience. No matter what type of trip you're looking for, Kharga Oasis offers something for everyone.

From outdoor activities and sightseeing to cultural exploration and relaxation, it's the perfect destination for a fun and memorable holiday.

Places to visit in Kharga Oasis

1. Dakhla Oasis: This is one of the most popular tourist destinations in the Kharga Oasis, located in the Western Desert of Egypt. It is known for its hot springs, beautiful palm-lined canals, and its ancient ruins. Visitors can enjoy a variety of activities such as camel rides, 4x4 dune bashing, and quad biking.

2. Temple of Hibis: This temple is located in the center of the Kharga Oasis and is a great place to explore the ancient culture and history of the region. Visitors can also enjoy a variety of activities such as camel rides, 4x4 dune bashing, and quad biking.

3. Kharga Museum: This museum is located in the center of the Kharga Oasis and offers visitors a great opportunity to learn about the history, art, and culture of the region. There are exhibits on the various cultures that have inhabited the region, as well as displays on the various archaeological sites in the area.

4. White Desert: This is a unique landscape of white chalk formations, located in the Western Desert of Egypt. Visitors can explore this area on a 4x4 safari and enjoy activities such as sand boarding and camel rides.

5. El-Bagawat Cemetery: This is one of the oldest and most interesting archaeological sites in the Kharga Oasis, located in the Western Desert of Egypt. Visitors can explore the tombs of the ancient Egyptians and learn about the burial customs of the time.

6. Dunqul Oasis: This is one of the most popular tourist destinations in the Kharga Oasis, located in the Western Desert of Egypt. It is known for its beautiful palm-lined canals and its ancient ruins. Visitors can enjoy a variety of activities such as camel rides, 4x4 dune bashing, and quad biking.

Suez

Suez is the perfect choice. With its stunning scenery, exciting activities, and vibrant culture, Suez is a great place to explore.

One of the top attractions in Suez is the Suez Canal, a historic waterway that connects the Mediterranean Sea and the Red Sea. Visitors can take a boat tour on the canal to learn about the history of the area and take in the beautiful scenery. There are also plenty of fishing and boating opportunities along the canal.

There are plenty of outdoor activities to enjoy in Suez. From hiking and mountain biking to camel riding and quad biking, there's something for everyone to enjoy. You can also explore the city's many parks and beaches, and take part in water sports such as windsurfing and kite surfing.

If you're looking to explore the culture of Suez, there are several interesting sites to visit. The Suez Museum is a great place to learn about the history and culture of the area, while the El-Gezira Park and the Suez Citadel are great places to explore the city's architecture.

The city also hosts a number of festivals throughout the year, including the Suez Festival of Music and Dance, which celebrates traditional music and dance from around the region.

Suez is a great destination for a fun and exciting vacation. With its beautiful scenery, exciting activities, and vibrant culture, it's the perfect place to explore and make lasting memories.

Places to visit in Suez

1. Suez Canal: A marvel of engineering, this historic waterway connects the Mediterranean and Red seas, offering visitors a chance to witness firsthand the history and beauty of the area.
2. Lake Timsah: A freshwater lake located in Suez, this is a great spot for swimming, boating, and fishing.
3. Suez Canal Museum: Learn about the history of the Suez Canal at this informative museum.
4. Beach of Suez: Take a dip in the Red Sea and enjoy the beautiful beaches of Suez.

5. Ras Mohammed National Park: This protected area is home to some of the best coral reefs in the world and is a great spot for snorkeling and diving.
6. The Grand Mosque of Suez: This 18th century mosque is a must-see for anyone interested in Islamic architecture and culture.
7. Port Tawfiq: This busy port is home to a variety of shops and restaurants, making it a great destination for a day of shopping and dining.
8. Hammam Faroun: This public bathhouse offers traditional Turkish baths, giving visitors a chance to relax and unwind.
9. Sand Dunes of Ras Sudr: Experience the beauty of the desert in this area of sand dunes and stunning views.
10. The Citadel of Suez: This 16th century fortress is a great spot to explore the history and culture of the area.

Ismailia

Ismailia is a beautiful city located in Egypt on the Suez Canal. It is known for its lush green gardens, stunning architecture, and relaxed atmosphere.

The city offers a variety of activities and attractions for visitors to enjoy. You can explore the vibrant markets of Ismailia, take a boat ride on the Suez Canal, or visit the beautiful lakes and parks. There are also plenty of cultural attractions to discover, such as the Ismailia Museum and the Ismailia Museum of Modern Art.

If you're looking for a unique activity, you can try a camel ride or go sandboarding on the nearby beaches. You can also go snorkeling or scuba diving in the water along the Suez Canal.

If you're looking for something a bit more relaxing, you can take a stroll through the beautiful gardens of Ismailia, or take in the city's unique architecture. There are also plenty of restaurants to choose from, so you can try out some of the local cuisine.

No matter what you're looking for, Ismailia has something for everyone. Whether you're looking for a few days of fun and adventure, or a relaxing getaway, you'll find it in Ismailia.

Places to visit in Ismailia

1. Suez Canal: The Suez Canal is a crucial international waterway that connects the Mediterranean Sea to the Red Sea and links Europe to Asia. The canal is a must-see destination when visiting Ismailia.

2. Ismailia Museum: The Ismailia Museum is one of the most important cultural institutions in the city. Located in the town center, the museum houses a collection of artifacts and information about the history of Ismailia and the region.

3. Lake Timsah: This large lake is a popular destination for swimming and other water activities. It is surrounded by a large park that includes a zoo, an aquarium, and other attractions.

4. El-Gisr Gardens: These beautiful gardens are located near the Ismailia Zoo and offer a peaceful retreat from the bustle of the city.

5. Ismailia Zoo: The Ismailia Zoo is home to a wide variety of animals, including lions, tigers, zebras, and more.

6. El Manzala Lagoon: This large lagoon is a popular destination for birdwatching and water sports.

7. Ismailia Old Town: This historic district is filled with narrow streets and traditional architecture. Visitors can explore the area and experience the unique culture of Ismailia.

8. Ismailia Desert: The desert surrounding Ismailia is an excellent destination for adventure activities such as desert safaris, quad biking, and camel rides.

Port Said

One of the most popular activities in Port Said is exploring the city's rich history. You can visit the old city of Port Said, where you can see historic monuments such as the Port Said Lighthouse, the Suez Canal Museum, and the Military Museum. These monuments provide a fascinating insight into the city's past and the people who have lived there.

Port Said also has plenty to offer. The city has several shopping centers, restaurants, and cafes. You can find everything from traditional Egyptian food to international cuisine. There are also plenty of boutiques and stores to explore, offering souvenirs, clothing, and other items.

When it comes to entertainment, Port Said has plenty to offer. There are several parks, gardens, and beaches, making it easy to take a break from your sightseeing and relax. The port of Port Said also offers boat tours and cruises, allowing visitors to experience the city from the water.

Also, Port Said is home to a vibrant nightlife scene. There are plenty of bars, clubs, and restaurants to choose from, making it easy to find a spot to let loose and have some fun.

Places to visit in Port Said

1. Port Said National Museum: This museum is located in the heart of Port Said, and it contains a wide range of artifacts from the city's history. It is a great place to learn more about the city and its culture.
2. Suez Canal Museum: This museum is located at the entrance of the Suez Canal and offers a unique look into the history of the canal. It contains a variety of artifacts and displays related to the canal's development and its importance to the region.
3. Kom el-Dikka: This archaeological site is located in the city center of Port Said and contains the remains of a large Roman villa. It is a great place to explore and learn about the history of this part of Egypt.
4. Corniche: This long promenade is located along the banks of the Suez Canal and offers great views of

the city. It is a great place to stroll around, relax, and take in the sights.

5. French Fort: This historic fort is located at the entrance of the Suez Canal and offers a great view of the canal. It is a great place to explore and learn more about the history of the area.

6. Fish Market: This popular market is located in the city center and is a great place to sample the local seafood. It is a great place to browse for souvenirs and pick up some local seafood for dinner.

CHAPTER FOUR

Conclusion

Egypt is an incredible country with a fascinating history that is well worth exploring.

From ancient monuments, vibrant cities, and beautiful beaches, there is something for everyone in this amazing country. Whether you are looking for a relaxing holiday or an adventurous journey, you will find that Egypt has something to offer.

With its warm climate, friendly locals, and abundant cultural attractions, Egypt is a great destination for any type of traveler. With its rich cultural heritage and vibrant energy, Egypt is a must-visit destination for anyone looking to experience the best that the Middle East has to offer. So, be sure to explore all that Egypt has to offer and experience the wonders of this incredible country.

Furthermore, Egypt is a country full of beauty, culture, and adventure. With its warm climate, friendly locals, and an abundance of attractions, it is the perfect destination for any type of traveler. From monuments and temples to beaches and markets, Egypt offers something for everyone. So, be sure to take a trip to Egypt and experience the wonders of this incredible country.

Thank you for reading and happy travels.

Printed in Great Britain
by Amazon

18455382R00047